from SEA TO SHINING SEA

ALASKA

By Dennis Brindell Fradin

CONSULTANTS

R.N. DeArmond, Sitka, editor and lifelong Alaska resident

Robert L. Hillerich, Ph.D., Professor Emeritus, Bowling Green State University;
Consultant, Pinellas County Schools, Florida

CHILDREN'S PRESS
A Division of Grolier Publishing
New York London Hong Kong Sydney
Danbury, Connecticut

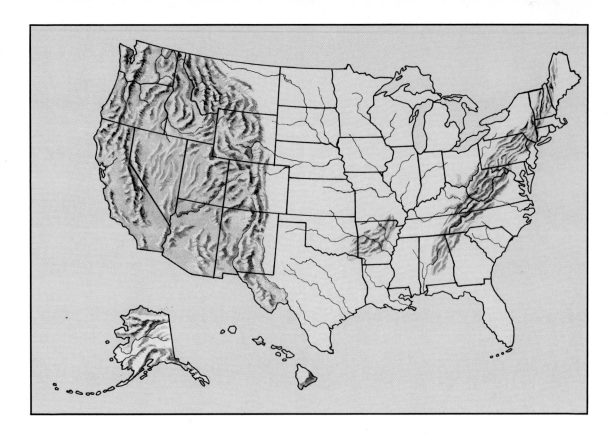

Alaska is the largest state in the United States.

For Emma Dryden

Front cover picture: Mount McKinley; page 1: mountain goats in Wrangell-St. Elias National Park;
back cover: dall sheep, Denali National Park

Project Editor: Joan Downing
Design Director: Karen Kohn
Research Assistant: Judith Bloom Fradin
Typesetting: Graphic Connections, Inc.
Engraving: Liberty Photoengraving

FOURTH PRINTING, 1994.

Library of Congress Cataloging-in-Publication Data

Fradin, Dennis B.
  Alaska / by Dennis Brindell Fradin.
    p.   cm. — (From sea to shining sea)
  Includes index.
  Summary: Introduces the history, geography, industry,
and people of the state known as the Last Frontier.
  ISBN 0-516-03802-8
  1. Alaska—Juvenile literature. [1. Alaska.] I. Title.
II. Series: Fradin, Dennis B. From sea to shining sea.
F904.3.F7   1993   93-15709
979.8—dc20   CIP
                                        AC

Table of Contents

A child enjoying the wildflowers in the Kenai Mountains near Seward

INTRODUCING THE LAST FRONTIER

Hawaii is the second state not bordered by other states.

Alaska is more than twice as big as Texas, the second-biggest state. It is nearly 500 times the size of Rhode Island, the smallest state.

Alaska is in the northwest corner of North America. It is the northernmost and westernmost of the fifty states. Alaska is one of two states not bordered by other states. It is only 50 miles from mainland Russia. The closest state is more than 500 miles away. Alaska is nicknamed the "Last Frontier."

The name *Alaska* comes from *alyeska*. This means "great land" in the language of Alaska's Aleut people. The name is fitting. It is by far the biggest state. North America's highest mountain is in Alaska. The world's largest bears live there. Alaska is tied with Texas as the top oil-producing state.

Much more is special about Alaska. Where were Benny Benson and Elizabeth Wanamaker Peratrovich born? Where is baseball played at midnight without lights? Where is the Iditarod Trail Sled Dog Race run each year? What state leads the

country in the value of fish caught? Where did North America's biggest earthquake occur? Where did North America's largest oil spill happen? The answer to these questions is: Alaska!

Overleaf: Mount McKinley

A picture map of Alaska

The Great Land

THE GREAT LAND

Alaska is the largest of the fifty states. It covers 591,004 square miles. Only 17 of the world's nearly 200 countries are larger.

Canada is the world's second-largest country. It borders eastern and southern Alaska. The Gulf of Alaska and the Pacific Ocean splash against Alaska to the south. The Bering Sea and Bering Strait touch Alaska's west coast. The Arctic Ocean forms Alaska's northern border.

Alaska's lowest points are along its oceans. They lie at sea level. The state's highest point is Mount McKinley. It is also the tallest peak in North America. Mount McKinley towers 20,320 feet above sea level. The sixteen highest mountains in the United States are all in Alaska.

About eighty of Alaska's mountains are volcanoes. Pavlof Volcano has erupted forty-one times since 1760.

Alaska also has about 100,000 glaciers. Most are along the south and southeast coasts. Malaspina Glacier is in southeast Alaska. It is the largest of these ice masses in North America. Malaspina Glacier covers 850 square miles.

An extinct volcano in Wrangell-St. Elias National Park

Alaska's 100,000 glaciers cover 30,000 square miles—an area the size of South Carolina.

Much of Alaska's land north of the Arctic Circle is treeless plain. It is called tundra. The land under this plain is permanently frozen. That is why trees do not grow there.

More than 1,800 islands are part of Alaska. Kodiak Island is the biggest. It is off the southern coast. Kodiak Island covers 3,588 square miles. The Aleutian Islands lie between the Bering Sea and the Pacific Ocean. They reach about 1,100 miles west of the mainland. Cape Wrangell on the Aleutians is the westernmost point in the United States.

Alaska has more than 3 million lakes. There are about 3,000 rivers. No other state has nearly that

The Arctic tundra

many. The largest lake is 1,150-square-mile Iliamna. The Yukon is Alaska's longest river. It flows 1,970 miles to the Bering Sea. The Yukon River starts in Canada. The Kuskokwim is Alaska's second-longest river. It flows for 724 miles.

CLIMATE

Parts of Alaska get the country's coldest winter temperatures. Winter readings below 0 degrees Fahrenheit are common. On January 23, 1971, the temperature fell to minus 80 degrees Fahrenheit at Prospect Creek. This was the country's all-time low temperature.

Icebergs in Portage Lake, Chugach National Forest

A forest in Katmai National Park

Southern Alaska is not as cold as the far north. A January day could be minus 30 degrees Fahrenheit at Barrow. That is in far northern Alaska. On the same day, Anchorage could be 20 degrees Fahrenheit. That is in the south. Alaskan winters are also snowy. Parts of the state receive 20 feet of snow a year.

Alaskan summers are cool. July temperatures in Fairbanks are about 60 degrees Fahrenheit. In Barrow, they are about 39 degrees Fahrenheit. The state's record-high temperature was 100 degrees Fahrenheit. This occurred at Fort Yukon on June 27, 1915. The east coast of Baranof Island gets about 221 inches of rain a year. In the United States, only Hawaii gets more.

Barrow is the country's coldest town or city. The yearly temperature there averages 9 degrees Fahrenheit.

11

Colorful wild plants and berries grow in the Arctic tundra.

Puffins are among the birds that live in Alaska.

Alaska is a windy state. Chinooks are warm winds. They can melt snow in mid-winter. Williwaws are sudden bursts of cold wind. They can reach speeds of 115 miles per hour.

One of Alaska's nicknames is "Land of the Midnight Sun." At the Arctic Circle, the sun does not set on June 21. Farther south, it sets for only a few hours on that day. From May 10 to August 2, the sun does not set at Barrow. There is daylight all that time. But from November 18 to January 24, Barrow has no sunlight. The sun does not rise there during that time.

PLANTS AND ANIMALS

A third of Alaska is wooded. The Sitka spruce is the state tree. This tree reaches 160-foot heights. Western hemlocks, willows, cottonwoods, cedars, aspens, and birches are other common trees. The forget-me-not is the state flower. It grows on the tundra and along streams.

Alaska has many kinds of wild animals. Alaska's brown bears are called Kodiak bears. They live on Kodiak Island. Kodiak bears are the world's largest bears. They weigh about 1,600 pounds. Polar bears live along the Arctic Ocean. Polar bears have been

seen swimming 50 miles from the nearest land or ice. Alaska also has grizzly bears and black bears.

Alaska's animals include caribou like this one (above).

Moose and caribou live in Alaska, too. About 8,000 wolves roam the state. Dall sheep climb the mountains. Alaska also has porcupines, beavers, mountain goats, foxes, and squirrels.

Alaska has about 450 kinds of birds. They include Arctic terns, puffins, loons, and geese. Alaska has more bald eagles than the other forty-nine states combined. The willow ptarmigan is the state bird.

The bald eagle is the country's official bird.

Alaskan waters are full of life, too. Whales and dolphins swim near the coast. Seals, walruses, and sea otters are found there, too.

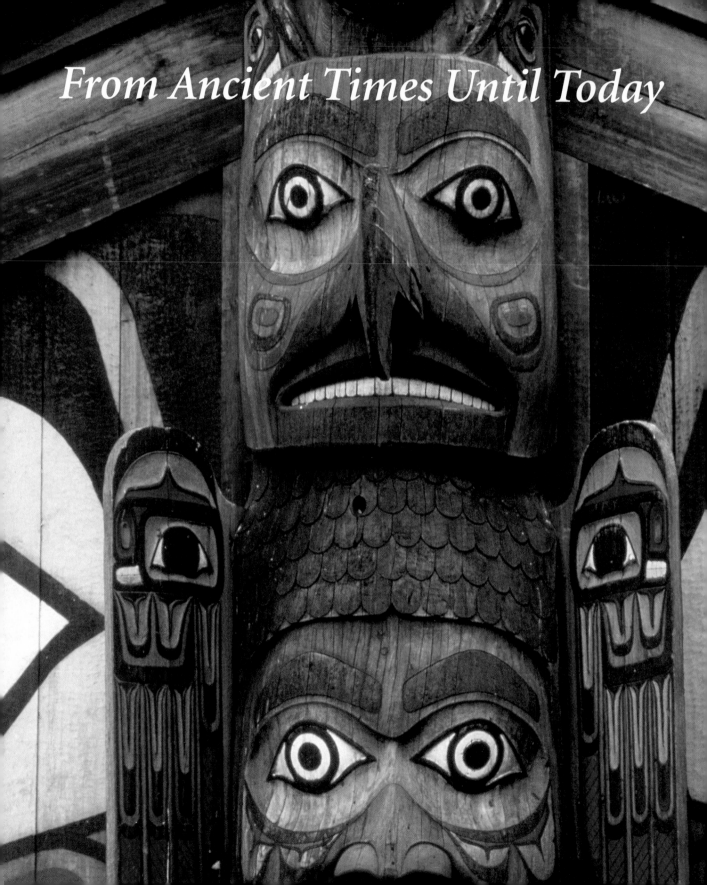

From Ancient Times Until Today

FROM ANCIENT TIMES UNTIL TODAY

About 2 million years ago, the Ice Age began. Glaciers covered far more of the state than they do now. Woolly mammoths roamed Alaska at that time. In 1986, this elephant-like animal was named the state fossil.

During the Ice Age, dry land linked Russia and Alaska. This is called the Bering Land Bridge. Between 20,000 and 50,000 years ago, people crossed the land bridge. They entered Alaska. From Alaska, they spread out across the Americas. About 14,000 years ago, the Bering Sea covered the land bridge.

AMERICAN INDIANS, ESKIMOS, AND ALEUTS

The first Alaskans were the Tlingit, Haida, and Athabascan Indians. The Tlingits and Haidas lived in the southeastern coastal forests. They fished for salmon and hunted deer. They also carved totem poles. These told a family's history. The Athabascans lived inland. They hunted moose. The Athabascans invented snowshoes. This made it easy for them to walk on top of snow.

Opposite page: A totem pole at Totem Bight Park, Ketchikan

Alaska's Athabascan Indians hunted moose like this one.

15

Eskimos lived in northern and western Alaska. They hunted seals from narrow boats called kayaks. They hunted whales from larger boats called umiaks. In winter, the Eskimos traveled over land by dog sled. The Eskimos word for home is *igloo*. Permanent homes were made of wood and dirt. Tents made from animal skins also were homes. Hunters far from home sometimes built igloos from blocks of snow.

The Aleuts were closely related to the Eskimos. They lived on the Aleutian Islands. The Aleuts also hunted whales. They built their homes with whale bones, dirt, and logs. The Aleuts made warm, hood-

This 1794 watercolor by Harry Humphrys shows a very large group of native Alaskan people in skin-covered canoes. They were fishing and trading in Cook Inlet.

ed coats from animal fur and skin. They called them parkas.

RUSSIAN AMERICA

Russia sent Vitus Bering to explore Alaska. Bering's crew landed on Alaska's Kayak Island in 1741. They became the first known Europeans on Alaskan soil.

The Bering Sea and Bering Strait were named for Vitus Bering.

Bering died before returning to Russia. But other members of his crew returned with valuable furs. Bering's men had hunted Alaskan sea otters and fur seals. Their furs could be made into clothing. Largely because of its furs, Alaska was claimed by Russia. It became known as Russian America.

Russian fur traders arrived in the Aleutian Islands in 1743. At that time, there were about 25,000 Aleuts. The Russians forced the Aleuts to kill sea otters for them. They also enslaved the Aleuts. The Aleuts rebelled against this treatment. Once, they burned several Russian ships. The Russians killed many Aleuts in revenge. By the late 1700s, only about 2,000 Aleuts remained.

In 1784, Grigory Shelikhov built Alaska's first Russian settlement. It was on Kodiak Island. Russian Orthodox priests came, too. They taught native Alaskans about Christianity.

Aleksandr Baranov began Sitka in 1804. For sixty years (1807-1867), Sitka was the capital of Russian America.

Many Russian men married native Alaskan women. A few brought their wives from Russia. Homes, schools, and churches sprang up in the little Russian settlements. The people grew vegetables and raised pigs and cattle. Yet, by 1867, only about 900 Russians lived in Russian America.

THE AMERICANS TAKE OVER

By the mid-1800s, Alaska's sea otters and fur seals had been overhunted. Russia started losing interest in Alaska. Meanwhile, the interest of fishing and mining companies in the United States grew.

On March 30, 1867, Secretary of State William Seward bought Alaska from Russia. The cost was $7.2 million. That was less than two cents an acre. But some Americans thought Alaska was a waste of money. They called Alaska "Seward's Folly" and "Seward's Icebox." On October 18, the United States flag was raised at Sitka. Today, two Alaskan holidays celebrate the change to United States rule. Seward's Day is the third Monday in March. Alaska Day is October 18.

William Seward

Alaska soon became a major center for catching salmon. Alaska's first salmon-canning factories opened in 1878.

In 1880, Joe Juneau and Dick Harris found gold in southeast Alaska. This set off Alaska's first big gold rush. The town that grew at the gold site was named Juneau.

In 1896, gold was found in Canada's Klondike area. That is just east of Alaska. This gold rush helped Alaska, too. Thousands of miners passed through Alaska on their way to the Klondike. Skagway and other Alaskan towns grew.

From 1899 to 1900, northwest Alaska had a gold rush. In 1899, Nome was founded. That is where the gold was discovered. The next year the *Nome Nugget* was begun. It is now the oldest newspaper in Alaska.

Gold was found in east-central Alaska in 1902. Once again, people rushed to the area. The miners called the place Fairbanks. It was named for Indiana lawmaker Charles Fairbanks. Fairbanks later became vice-president of the United States (1905-1909).

Gold mining and fishing boosted Alaska's population. In 1880, about 33,000 people lived there. By 1910, the population had almost doubled to about 64,000.

Joseph Juneau

THE ALASKA TERRITORY: 1912-1959

A territory is land owned by a country. With a capital "T," such as Alaska Territory, it means a region that is owned by a country and that has its own government.

The gold rushes also caught Congress's attention in Washington, D. C. In 1884, Alaska received a governor. Alaskans sent a delegate to the United States Congress in 1906.

In 1912, the United States Congress finally made Alaska a territory. This was a move toward statehood. Alaskans could have their own legislature. Juneau became the capital. Alaska's territorial legislature met in 1913. The first law it passed gave Alaskan women the vote. Most women in the United States couldn't vote until 1920.

Alaska was huge. It had many remote areas. Alaskans needed better ways to get around this land. The first airplane flight in Alaska took place in 1913. Hundreds of small airports were built in

This 1913 picture shows the first airplane to fly in Alaska.

Alaska over the years. Work began on the Alaska Railroad in 1915. By 1923, it linked Fairbanks to the southern coast. Many roads were cut through to hard-to-reach places.

In 1943, American troops landed on Attu and drove the Japanese from the island.

In 1929, the Great Depression (1929-1939) hit the United States. People were out of work. Times were hard. Many Americans looking for jobs moved to Alaska. The United States government settled 200 farm families in the Matanuska Valley. This is north of Anchorage. The land there is good for farming.

In 1941, the United States entered World War II (1939-1945). The next year, Japan seized the Aleutian islands of Attu and Kiska. This was the only invasion of United States soil in the war. In 1943, the United States drove the enemy from these islands. About 2,500 Japanese and 600 Americans died during the Battle of Attu.

Several United States military bases were built in Alaska during the war. They included Elmendorf Air Force Base and Fort Richardson. Both are near Anchorage. More than 150,000 United States troops were stationed in Alaska. In 1942, the Alaska-Canada Military Highway (Alcan) was built. It served as a wartime supply route. This 1,400-mile highway was built in just eight months.

World War II was won in 1945. Many soldiers and wartime workers had grown to love Alaska. They moved there after the war. Alaska's population had been 73,000 in 1940. By 1959, it had tripled to more than 200,000. That year, on January 3, Alaska became the forty-ninth state. Juneau was the capital. William Egan was Alaska's first state governor.

Alaskans celebrated statehood at a July 4, 1959, ceremony.

GROWTH OF THE FORTY-NINTH STATE

In 1963, the Marine Highway System opened. This is a network of ferryboats. They link mainland and island cities on Alaska's southern coasts. Today, about 500,000 passengers use the Marine Highway System each year.

Soon after the state's fifth birthday, disaster struck. The date was March 27, 1964—Good Friday. That afternoon an earthquake rocked southern Alaska. It was the strongest one ever measured in North America. In Anchorage, buildings toppled. The quake also set off giant waves. Thirty people on a dock at Valdez were washed out to sea. The Good Friday Earthquake killed 131 people.

In 1968, oil was found at Prudhoe Bay. It is North America's largest known oil field. Prudhoe Bay is in far northern Alaska. The oil had to be piped to the south. In 1974, work began on the Alaska Pipeline. Thousands of people came to build the 800-mile-long pipeline. It was completed in

The 1964 earthquake caused the collapse of this Anchorage street. A tidal wave set off by the quake even killed several people in California.

1977. The pipeline stretches from Prudhoe Bay to Valdez.

The pipeline made oil a giant industry in Alaska. By 1980, Alaska was producing nine times as much oil as in 1976. The mining of natural gas became important in the late 1980s. People from other states came to work in Alaska's oil and gas industries. Between 1970 and 1990, Alaska's population nearly doubled.

On Good Friday, March 24, 1989, disaster hit Alaska again. The oil tanker *Exxon Valdez* hit a reef off southern Alaska. About 11 million gallons of oil gushed into Prince William Sound. This was the biggest oil spill in North America. The oil killed about 300,000 birds. It also killed many sea otters and seals.

A huge cleanup project was begun. Thousands of people cleaned Alaska's beaches. They also rescued oil-soaked animals. The beaches are returning to normal. But some kinds of fish and birds may have suffered lasting damage.

As the year 2000 approaches, Alaska faces problems. The state's motto is "North to the Future." Many people have moved there seeking better lives. Now, Alaska does not have enough jobs to go around. By 1993, about one-tenth of the state's

Oil from the Exxon Valdez *spill spread more than 1,000 miles along Alaska's shore. The people shown here are working to clean up some of the mess.*

workers were jobless. Many out-of-work Alaskans are very poor. Alaska's Native Americans have been especially hard hit.

Alaskans can't agree about how to create more jobs and industries. Five-sixths of Alaska is public land. This includes parklands and forests. Some Alaskans want these lands opened to oil drilling. Others say that public lands must always be protected. The battle over land will continue to be a big issue for years to come.

The Alaska Pipeline was completed in 1977.

Overleaf: A costumed Chilkat dancer, in Haines

Alaskans and Their Work

ALASKANS AND THEIR WORK

The United States Census counted 550,043 Alaskans in 1990. Wyoming is the only state with fewer people. Alaska is the least crowded state. The Last Frontier averages less than one person per square mile. New Jersey has 1,000 people per square mile. It is the most crowded state.

THE ALASKANS

Alaskans live far from the rest of the United States. Because of this, they have developed special ways. Alaskans tend to think of the world as having two parts. There is Alaska. Then, there is everywhere else. Alaskans call that the "Outside." Alaskans have nicknamed the rest of the United States. They call it the "Lower 48." That includes all the other states except Hawaii.

Three of every four Alaskans are white. Their families came from dozens of countries. Large numbers are of German, English, and Irish backgrounds.

One-sixth of all Alaskans are Native Americans. That is a higher rate than any other state. About

About 75 percent of Alaskans are white. Nearly 16 percent are Native Americans.

Costumed Norwegian children dancing at the Petersburg docks

Hispanic people are of Spanish-speaking ancestry.

45,000 Alaskans are Eskimos. About 10,000 are Aleuts. Another 12,000 are Tlingit Indians. The rest belong to other Indian groups.

Three groups of Alaskans are growing rapidly. Between 1980 and 1990, the number of Asian Alaskans more than doubled. Many of these 20,000 people came from the Philippines and Korea. During those years, the number of black Alaskans nearly doubled to 22,000. Likewise, the state's Hispanic population nearly doubled to 18,000. Many Hispanic Alaskans trace their roots to Mexico.

ALASKANS AT WORK

About 276,000 Alaskans have jobs. That is nearly half the state's people. Government work is the most popular kind of job. One-third of Alaska's 75,000 government workers are in the military. The state has forty-five military bases or offices. Public school teachers are also counted among the government workers.

About 60,000 Alaskans do service work. Doctors, nurses, and lawyers are service workers. People who fix cars and airplanes are also service workers. Some Alaskans own their own small planes.

Left: A naturalist lecturing on an Alaska State Ferry boat
Right: A pilot flying over Gates of the Arctic National Park

One Alaskan in sixty is a pilot. That is the highest rate in the country.

They live far from towns. They fly their airplanes to town like people elsewhere drive their cars. About 50,000 Alaskans sell goods. Many small towns have just one store. Service workers in Alaska are very important.

Nearly 16,000 Alaskans make products. Food is the state's leading product. Salmon and other fish are packaged in Alaska. Oil refining is another big industry.

Some coal is also mined in Alaska. This is the Usibelli Coal Mine, in Healy.

About 12,000 Alaskans work in mining. Oil is the state's top mining product. Alaska and Texas are tied as the top oil-producing states. Alaska is also a major producer of natural gas, gold, silver, and lead. The state ranks first in mining zinc.

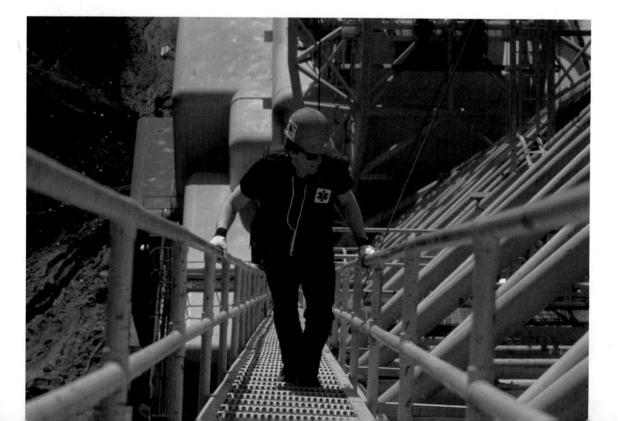

Only a few thousand Alaskans fish for a living. But Alaska is the top fishing state. About 6 *billion* pounds of fish and other seafood are caught yearly in Alaskan waters. This amounts to a pound for every person on earth. Salmon is the top catch. Shrimp, crabs, and halibut are also important.

Alaska has only 600 farms. That is the fewest of any state. Alaska's farmers raise dairy cows, beef cattle, chickens, and sheep. They grow potatoes, hay, and barley. Alaskan vegetables can reach great sizes. Cabbages sometimes weigh 95 pounds. Carrots the size of baseball bats have been grown there.

Left: A crab fisherman unloading his catch in Haines
Right: People who fish for sport often catch halibut.

Overleaf: Fireworks over Anchorage

A Trip Through the Last Frontier

A Trip Through the Last Frontier

Alaska has much to see that no other state can offer. Visitors can see North America's highest peak and the "midnight sun." They also visit Eskimo villages and glaciers.

Panhandle and Southern Coast

Totem poles at the Totem Heritage Cultural Center in Ketchikan

Southeast Alaska is called the Panhandle. It is a long strip of land with many islands. No highways link the cities of Alaska's Panhandle. There, people travel the area by boat or airplane. Alaska has "air taxi" operators. They fly people from place to place.

Ketchikan is near the lower end of the Panhandle. Ketchikan calls itself the "Salmon Capital of the World." Fishing fleets bring back salmon and other fish to Ketchikan. Ketchikan is also known for its totem poles. The Totem Heritage Cultural Center has dozens of these poles.

Sitka is about halfway up the Panhandle. With 8,500 people, Sitka is Alaska's fourth biggest city in population. In area, it is the country's largest city. Sitka covers 4,700 square miles. That is about the size of Connecticut.

Sitka was the capital of Russian America. St. Michael's Cathedral is a rebuilt Russian church. It looks like the one built in 1848. Long ago, Russian religious leaders lived in a log building. It was called the Russian Bishop's House. Today, it is open to visitors.

About 100 miles to the north is Juneau. This is Alaska's capital. It is the only state capital that can't be reached by road. The Alaska legislature meets in the state capitol. The Alaska State Museum is another highlight of Juneau. There are displays on Eskimos, Aleuts, and Athabascans. Visitors also learn about the state's mining and fishing history at the museum.

*Left: Ketchikan
Right: A life-size bronze bear sculpture and the Alaska State Capitol*

Besides being Alaska's capital, Juneau is its third biggest city. About 27,000 people live there.

35

Muir Glacier, in Glacier Bay National Park

About forty glaciers are in the Juneau area. Mendenhall Glacier is partly in the city. Juneau people call it their "backyard glacier."

Some people come to Alaska to see its national parks. Eight of the country's fifty national parks are in Alaska. Five are along the southern coast.

Glacier Bay National Park is in the northern Panhandle. Visitors can see huge pieces of glaciers fall into the water. These are known as icebergs. Visitors also go to the park to watch whales.

The country's biggest national park is in southeast Alaska. Wrangell-St. Elias National Park covers

13,000 square miles. Glaciers and tall mountains are highlights of this park.

Alaska has many fjords. These are fingers of the sea that extend inland. Kenai Fjords National Park is near Seward. Sea otters, seals, and puffins live at the park.

West of Kenai Peninsula is Lake Clark National Park. It is on the southwest coast. Bald eagles and grizzly bears catch fish there.

About 100 miles to the south is Katmai National Park. The park's fifteen volcanoes include Novarupta. It erupted in 1912. The blast lasted for sixty hours. The park's rivers are often filled with salmon. At those times, their waters look red.

Exit Glacier, Seward

Kodiak Island is east of Katmai. Kodiak National Wildlife Refuge covers most of the island. People go there to see the huge Kodiak bears.

ANCHORAGE

The city of Anchorage was begun in 1914 as a construction camp for the Alaska Railroad.

Anchorage is Alaska's biggest city. It lies in the middle of the southern coast. Anchorage began in 1914 as a railroad town. Today, more than 225,000 people live there. No other Alaskan city has one-seventh as many people. Almost half of all Alaskans live in Anchorage.

In many ways, Anchorage is like big cities in the Lower 48. Anchorage has tall office buildings. The

The Performing Arts Center, Anchorage

Performing Arts Center has concerts, ballets, and

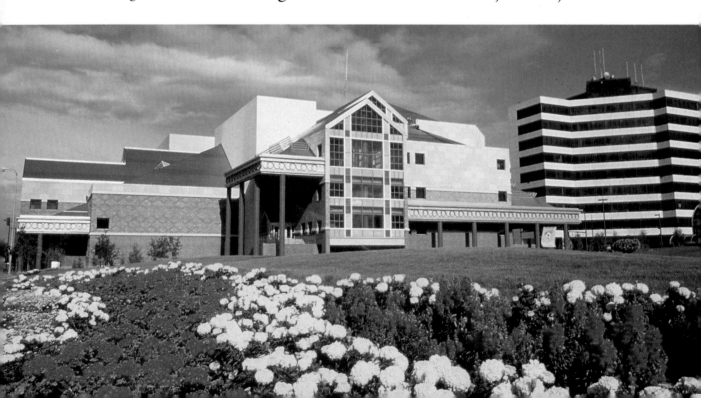

operas. The Anchorage Museum of History and Art has artworks by Alaskans.

Yet, in some ways, Anchorage is unlike other big United States cities. There is an amazing amount of wildlife in and near Anchorage. About 1,000 wild moose can be found within the city. They cross highways. Sometimes they enter shopping centers. Bears, too, enter Anchorage at times. At least one wolf pack roams Chugach State Park.

Alaska's official state sport is sled dog racing. It is also called mushing. The person who drives the dog team is called the musher. The Iditarod is the most famous of these races. Each March the Iditarod Trail Sled Dog Race starts in Anchorage. It ends 1,100 miles later in Nome.

Anchorage may have the country's only Northern Lights Boulevard. It was named for a natural light show in Alaska's night sky. Activity on the sun causes the northern lights. They often appear in the sky as curtains of colored light. The northern lights occur in the spring and fall.

The Iditarod Trail Sled Dog Race starts in Anchorage.

The northern lights are also called the aurora borealis.

HIGHLIGHTS OF CENTRAL AND WESTERN ALASKA

Mount McKinley is north of Anchorage. It is in Denali National Park. *Denali* is an Athabascan word

Hikers on Kahiltna Glacier, Mount McKinley

meaning "the great one." Thousands of visitors have climbed to the top of Mount McKinley. Others have died trying.

North of Denali is Nenana. Each spring the town holds the Nenana Ice Classic. People bet on when the ice will break apart on the Tanana River. In 1995, the ice broke at 1:22 P.M. on April 26. One dozen Alaskans split the $330,000 jackpot.

Farther north is Fairbanks. About 30,000 people live there. It is Alaska's second largest city. Fairbanks began in 1902 as a gold-mining center.

ie "Golden Heart of Alaska."

hundreds of miles to shop in

ller towns do not have all the

y of Alaska was founded in

Today, it has three main branch-

chorage, Juneau, and Fairbanks.

Alaska Museum is in Fairbanks.

i's wildlife and Native Americans

shing Museum is also in Fairbanks.

e to learn about sled dog racing.

two races each winter. One is the

nerican Open Sled Dog Championship.

*The University of
Alaska Museum, in
Fairbanks*

The other is the 1,000-mile Yukon Quest. It ends in Whitehorse in Canada's Yukon Territory.

Fairbanks hosts a famous baseball game on June 21. This is the Midnight Sun Game. The first pitch is thrown at 11 P.M. The game ends around 2 A.M. The game is played without lights.

About 450 miles west of Fairbanks is Nome. Long ago this area had no name. A mapmaker wrote *name?* for the area. He didn't know what to call it. On the finished map, it came out *Nome*. In 1925, Nome had an outbreak of diphtheria. Medicine was brought by dog sled from Nenana. That is 650 miles away. Hundreds of lives were saved. Today, the Iditarod finishes at Nome. Part of the race follows the path used in 1925.

More than half of Nome's 3,500 people are Eskimos. The Carrie McLain Museum in Nome displays Eskimo art. It also has displays on Nome's gold rush. Gold is still mined around Nome. Visitors can pan for gold on Nome's beaches. They may keep any they find.

An Eskimo dancer at the Chevak Tanquik Theater, in far western Alaska

ALASKA'S ARCTIC

The Arctic Circle marks Alaska's northern third. Most of this northern land is tundra. No trees grow

there. In the spring, however, wildflowers cover the ground. Few people live in the Alaskan Arctic.

Kotzebue is 25 miles above the Arctic Circle. It is in northwest Alaska. Kotzebue is a famous Eskimo village. The Museum of the Arctic has Eskimo crafts on display. There, visitors can join in an Eskimo game of blanket toss. Long ago, Eskimo hunters found a way to spot faraway animals. Using a blanket, they would toss a hunter high into the air. The blanket was made of walrus skin. The hunter

Left: Inupiat Eskimo children in Kotzebue
Right: A blanket toss in Barrow

could see a long way from up there. This turned into the game of blanket toss. Non-Eskimos now play blanket toss, too. Several people form a circle. They toss the person on the blanket about 20 feet into the air. It feels like bouncing on a trampoline.

Kobuk Valley National Park is east of Kotzebue. It is close to where the Bering Land Bridge used to be. This park has two large sand dunes. Grizzly bears and wolves live in the park.

Gates of the Arctic National Park is east of Kobuk Valley. It has no roads or paths. It is one of the country's few large areas of total wilderness.

Canoeing on Narvak Lake, in Gates of the Arctic National Park

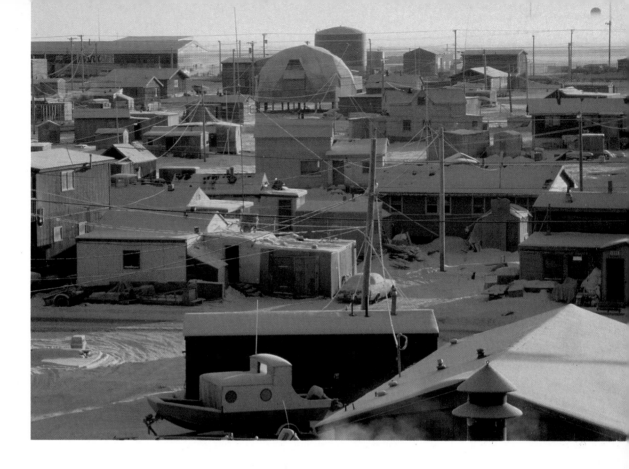

The park's Arctic scenery includes mountains and lakes.

A view of Barrow

Arctic National Wildlife Refuge is in Alaska's far northeast corner. The animals that live there are protected from hunters. These animals include wolves, moose, caribou, and grizzly bears.

Barrow is a good place to end an Alaska trip. It is a large Eskimo town. It is also the northernmost town in the United States. Visitors shop for Eskimo masks and dolls. Barrow is the best place to see the midnight sun. There is sunlight from May 10 until August 2.

Yukon Delta National Wildlife Refuge is in southwest Alaska. It is the largest United States national wildlife refuge— slightly larger than Arctic National Wildlife Refuge.

A Gallery of Famous Alaskans

A GALLERY OF FAMOUS ALASKANS

Sheldon Jackson

Opposite page: Ernest Gruening

Many interesting people have had ties with Alaska. They include explorers, lawmakers, and the boy who created Alaska's flag.

Vitus Bering (1681-1741) was born in Denmark. He joined the Russian navy as a young man. Bering sailed to Alaska for Russia (1728 and 1741). People once thought that Asia and North America were connected. On his first trip, Bering proved that the two continents were separate. He sailed through what is now called the Bering Strait. On his second trip, he discovered the Aleutian Islands. Bering became the first European to land in Alaska.

Sheldon Jackson (1834-1909) was born in New York State. He became a Christian missionary. Jackson made twenty-six trips to Alaska. He taught the native peoples about Christ. Jackson also opened free schools for the native peoples. Sitka's Sheldon Jackson College and Sheldon Jackson Museum were named for him.

Carl Ben Eielson (1897-1929) was born in North Dakota. He was a pilot during World War I.

Alaska's Mt. Eielson as well as Eielson Air Force Base near Fairbanks were named for Carl Ben Eielson (below).

Jay Hammond served two terms and was one of Alaska's most popular governors.

Eielson came to Alaska in 1922. He taught at Fairbanks High School. Soon he bought an airplane. He became a famous Alaskan "bush pilot." Eielson flew people and supplies into remote areas. In 1928, he and explorer Hubert Wilkins flew from Barrow, Alaska. They landed on the Norwegian island of Spitsbergen. That was a 2,200-mile flight across the Arctic Ocean. Eielson and Wilkins were the first to do that. In 1929, Eielson's plane crashed and he died. Eielson was on his way to help a Russian ship that was stuck in the ice.

Jefferson Randolph Smith (1860-1898) was born in Georgia. He was known as "Soapy" Smith. Smith came to Skagway in 1897. He became Alaska's most famous "bad guy." He ran a gambling hall. There, he cheated miners out of their gold. Meanwhile, Smith's gang went around picking people's pockets. Smith also opened a "telegraph office" in Skagway. He charged five dollars to send a message home for miners. But Smith just pretended to send their messages. Alaska had no telegraph yet. Smith's days of cheating soon came to an end. He was shot and killed during a fight.

Jay Hammond was born in New York State in 1922. He became a scientist. During World War II, he was a pilot. In 1946, he moved to Alaska. Like

Carl Ben Eielson, Hammond became a bush pilot. He also served in the Alaska legislature for about ten years. Then Hammond became Alaska's governor (1974-1982).

Ann Coleman (1872-1973) was born in Kentucky. She came to Alaska in 1912. For many years, she worked as Juneau's city librarian. Children who used the library loved her. Coleman retired when she was about seventy-five. She died in a Pioneers' Home.

Elizabeth Wanamaker Peratrovich (1911-1958) was born in Sitka. She was a Tlingit Indian. Peratrovich became president of the Alaska Native Sisterhood. This group worked for Native Alaskans' rights. They were denied their rights for many years.

49

They couldn't vote until 1924. Their children were kept apart from white schoolchildren until 1949. Hotels and restaurants had signs saying NO NATIVES ALLOWED. In 1945, Peratrovich made a famous speech to Alaska lawmakers. They then passed a law. It gave Native Alaskans equal treatment in public places.

Ernest Gruening (1887-1974) was the governor who signed that 1945 law. Gruening was born in New York City. He earned a degree as a medical doctor. But he worked for many years as a reporter

Benny Benson holds up the Alaska flag he designed for the Alaska Territory. It is now Alaska's official state flag.

and editor. In 1939, he was made Alaska's territorial governor. Gruening helped convince the U.S. Congress to make Alaska a state. After statehood, he served as a U.S. senator from Alaska (1959-1969). Gruening also wrote several books about Alaska.

Benny Benson (1913-1972) was born at Chignik. That is in southern Alaska. He grew up in a Seward orphanage. When Benson was thirteen, he entered a contest to design Alaska's flag. His design showed eight stars on a blue background. It won the contest. "The blue field is for the Alaska sky and the forget-me-not, an Alaska flower," Benny wrote. "The North Star is for the future state of Alaska, the most northerly of the Union. The dipper [the other seven stars] is for the Great Bear—symbolizing strength." Benson's flag flew over the Alaska Territory for many years. Then, in 1959, it became the state flag. As an adult, Benson worked as an airplane mechanic in Kodiak.

The group of stars called the Big Dipper is also known as the Great Bear.

Marie Drake (1888-1963) was from Ohio. She moved to Alaska as a young woman. Drake worked in Alaska's Education Department. In 1935, she wrote a poem called "Alaska's Flag." It was set to music. Later, it became Alaska's state song.

Walter Hickel was born in Kansas in 1919. He moved to Alaska when he was about twenty. Hickel

The secretary of the interior is in charge of some United States public lands and other natural resources.

arrived there with thirty-seven cents in his pocket. Hickel became wealthy. He built and owned hotels and shopping centers. In 1966, he became Alaska's second state governor. Partway through his term, Hickel was named U.S. secretary of the interior. He was the first Alaskan in a U.S. president's cabinet. In 1990, Hickel was again elected governor of Alaska.

Ron Dalby was born in Skagway in 1949. He edited *Alaska* magazine. He has written three books about Alaska. One of them is about the Alaska Highway. Dalby and his family have taken about twenty trips on that road. Now, he works as a bush pilot.

Susan Butcher is the most famous Iditarod champion. She was born in Massachusetts in 1954. In 1973, Butcher read about Alaska's first Iditarod. Two years later, she moved to Alaska. She began preparing for the Iditarod. Butcher lived in a remote area. There, she hunted for food and trained her dogs. She finished nineteenth in her first Iditarod in 1978. Butcher was leading in 1985. She dropped out when a moose attacked her dogs. That year, Libby Riddles won the race. Butcher kept coming back. She won the Iditarod in 1986, 1987, 1988, and 1990. Butcher was the first musher to win the Iditarod three years straight.

Birthplace of Benny Benson, Elizabeth Wanamaker Peratrovich, and Ron Dalby . . .

Home to Susan Butcher, Carl Ben Eielson, and Walter Hickel . . .

Site of North America's tallest mountain, biggest glacier, and greatest number of active volcanoes . . .

Today, a leader at producing oil and catching fish . . .

The only place in the country where baseball is played at midnight without lights . . .

This is the country's Last Frontier—Alaska!

Jeff King was the 1993 Iditarod winner.

Did You Know?

The country's tallest snowman was built in Anchorage in 1988 by a team led by Myron Ace. "Super Frosty" stood 63.5 feet tall.

Taras Genet of Talkeetna became the youngest person to climb Mount McKinley. He did so in 1991 at the age of twelve.

The Alaskan malamute is a large sled dog. The malamute originated in Alaska 3,000 years ago.

England, France, Germany, and Switzerland could fit together inside Alaska.

Northernmost Alaska is 1,300 miles from the North Pole. However, Alaska does have a town called North Pole, near Fairbanks. Many letters addressed to Santa Claus go there.

Other Alaskan towns with unusual names include Clam Gulch, Candle, Beaver, Chicken, Deadhorse, King Salmon, Red Devil, and Eek.

The Kuskokwim River freezes so solid in the winter that cars and trucks use it as a highway.

Balto was one of the dogs who helped bring medicine to Nome in 1925. In New York City's Central Park, there is a statue of Balto.

The country's highest zip code is 99950. That is the code for Coffman Cove in southeast Alaska.

The farthest "line of sight" in the United States is in Alaska. Mount McKinley can be spotted from Alaska's Mount Sanford, 230 miles away.

Eskimo ice cream is popular in Alaska. It is made with snow, seal oil, and whipped berries.

Strange things happen in Alaska's very cold winters. At minus 40 degrees Fahrenheit, people's breath turns to ice crystals. Alaska also has winter "ice fog." It is made of tiny pieces of ice rather than water droplets, as in ordinary fog.

Alaskans are wild about baseball. Alaska has two baseball leagues for major-league hopefuls. The teams include the Fairbanks Goldpanners, the North Pole Nicks, and the Anchorage Glacier Pilots. Alaska's leagues have sent 150 players to the big leagues. They include pitcher Tom Seaver and slugger Dave Winfield.

On May 17, 1985, the largest salmon on record was caught in Alaska's Kenia River. Les Anderson's famous salmon weighed 97 pounds, 4 ounces.

Valdez, in south-central Alaska, was moved 4 miles west. The town was so badly damaged by the 1964 Good Friday Earthquake that it was rebuilt on a new site.

Alaska has many small schools. Each June, about twenty-five Alaska high schools graduate just one student.

Athabascan chief Walter Northway celebrated his 116th birthday in June 1992.

ALASKA INFORMATION

State flag

Forget-me-nots

Area: 591,004 square miles (the largest of the fifty states)

Greatest Distance North to South: 1,350 miles

Greatest Distance East to West: 2,350 miles

Borders: The Arctic Ocean to the north; the Bering Sea, with the Bering Strait separating Alaska from Russia, to the west; the Pacific Ocean and the Gulf of Alaska to the south; the Yukon Territory to the east; and British Columbia to the east and south

Highest Point: Mount McKinley, 20,320 feet above sea level (the highest peak in North America)

Lowest Point: Sea level, along Alaska's coastline

Hottest Recorded Temperature: 100° F. (at Fort Yukon, on June 27, 1915)

Coldest Recorded Temperature: -80° F. (at Prospect Creek, on January 23, 1971; the record low temperature for the United States)

Statehood: The forty-ninth state, on January 3, 1959

Origin of Name: *Alaska* comes from *alyeska,* an Aleut word meaning "great land" or "mainland"

Capital: Juneau

United States Representatives: 1 (as of 1992)

State Senators: 20

State Representatives: 40

State Song: "Alaska's Flag," by Marie Drake (words) and Elinor Dusenbury (music)

State Motto: "North to the Future"

Nicknames: "Last Frontier," "Land of the Midnight Sun"

State Seal: Adopted 1913   **State Flower:** Forget-me-not

State Flag: Adopted 1927   **State Bird:** Willow ptarmigan

State Tree: Sitka spruce

State Sea Animal: Bowhead whale

State Fish: King salmon

State Gem: Jade

State Mineral: Gold

State Fossil: Woolly mammoth

State Sport: Dog mushing

Sitka spruce

Mountains: Alaska has the sixteen highest peaks in the United States: Mt. McKinley, Mt. St. Elias, Mt. Foraker, Mt. Bona, Mt. Blackburn, Mt. Sanford, Mt. Vancouver, South Buttress, Mt. Churchill, Mt. Fairweather, Mt. Hubbard, Mt. Bear, East Buttress , Mt. Hunter, Browne Tower, Mt. Alverstone

Some Rivers: Yukon, Kuskokwim, Tanana, Koyukuk, Sustina, Matanuska, Porcupine, Colville, Noatak, Copper

Some Lakes: Iliamna, Aleknagik, Becharof, Clark, Selawik

Some Islands: Kodiak, Prince of Wales, Chichagof, Saint Lawrence, Admiralty, Revillagigedo, Baranof

Wildlife: Kodiak bears, black bears, polar bears, grizzly bears, moose, elk, caribou, black-tailed deer, wolves, Dall's sheep, mountain goats, musk oxen, beavers, porcupines, foxes, wolverines, muskrats, river otters, weasels, snowshoe hares, sea otters, willow ptarmigans, Arctic terns, puffins, loons, geese, bald eagles, many other kinds of birds, whales, dolphins, fur seals, salmon, halibut, clams, cod, crabs, shrimp, herring

Manufactured Products: Packaged salmon, herring, crab, other foods, refined oil, lumber

Farm Products: Milk, beef cattle, chickens, eggs, sheep, reindeer, potatoes, hay, barley, oats

Mining Products: Oil, natural gas, zinc, gold, silver, lead, coal

Fishing Products: Salmon, shrimp, crabs, halibut, herring, cod

Population: 551,947, the least populated state except for Wyoming (1990 U.S. Census Bureau figures)

Major Cities (1990 Census):

Anchorage	226,338	Ketchikan	8,263
Fairbanks	30,843	Kodiak	6,365
Juneau	26,751	Kenai	6,327
Sitka	8,588		

Willow ptarmigan

Polar bear

ALASKA HISTORY

48,000-18,000 B.C.—The first people reach Alaska

1741—Vitus Bering, exploring for Russia, lands on Kayak Island

1743—Russian hunters and fur traders arrive

1784—Grigory Shelikhov builds Alaska's first Russian settlement on Kodiak Island

1807—Sitka becomes the capital of Russian America

1853—The first oil in Alaska is discovered in Cook Inlet

1867—On March 30, U.S. Secretary of State William Seward buys Alaska from Russia

1868—Alaska's first newspaper, the *Sitka Times,* is begun

1878—Alaska's first salmon canneries open

1880—Juneau is founded on the site of a gold discovery by Joe Juneau and Dick Harris

1896—Gold found in Canada's Klondike area aids the growth of Alaska

1899—Gold is found in Nome

1900—The *Nome Nugget,* now Alaska's oldest newspaper, is begun

1902—Fairbanks begins as a gold rush town

1910—Alaska's population is 64,356

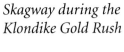

Skagway during the Klondike Gold Rush

1912—Novarupta Volcano erupts; Congress makes Alaska a
    territory

1913—The Alaska Territory's legislature first meets; women in
    Alaska are given the right to vote

1914—Anchorage is founded

1915—Work begins on the Alaska Railroad

1917—The University of Alaska is founded in Fairbanks

1923—The Alaska Railroad is completed, linking Seward and
    Fairbanks

1942—Japan seizes the Alaskan islands of Attu and Kiska during
    World War II; the Alaska Highway is built

1943—U.S. forces drive the Japanese from Attu and Kiska

1945—The United States and its allies win World War II

1950—Alaska's population reaches 128,643

1959—Alaska becomes the forty-ninth state on January 3

1964—On March 27, the Good Friday Earthquake strikes south-
    central Alaska, causing 131 deaths and $500 million in
    damages

1968—North America's largest known oil field is found at
    Alaska's Prudhoe Bay

1969—Walter Hickel, Alaska's governor, becomes U.S. secretary
    of the interior

1973—The Iditarod Trail Sled Dog Race has its first run

1977—The Alaska oil pipeline is completed

1989—The *Exxon Valdez* runs aground, spilling 11 million gallons
    of oil in Prince William Sound

1990—The Last Frontier's population reaches 551,947

1991—Walter Hickel becomes Alaska's governor again

1995—Doug Swingly of Montana is the first non-Alaskan to win
    the Iditarod; Tony Knowles takes office as governor

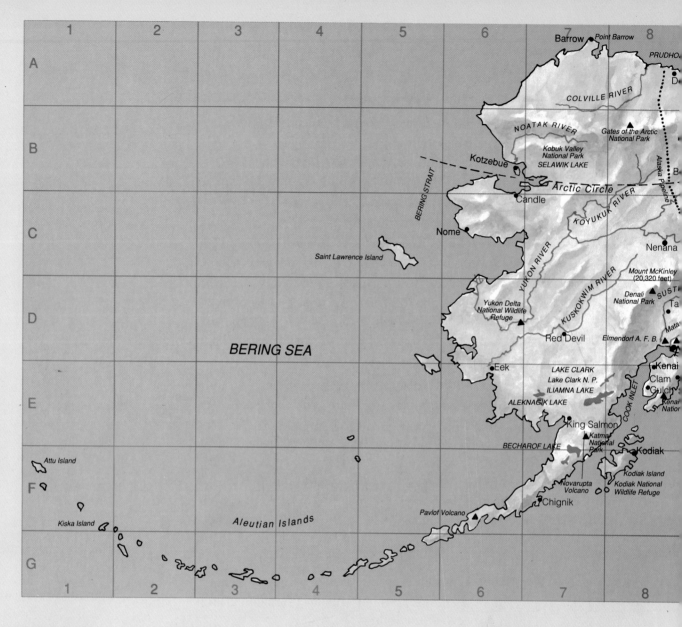

Map labels (on map):

Barrow • Point Barrow

PRUDHO...

COLVILLE RIVER

NOATAK RIVER

Gates of the Arctic National Park

Kobuk Valley National Park

SELAWIK LAKE

Kotzebue

Alaska Pipeline

Arctic Circle

Candle

KOYUKUK RIVER

Nenana

Nome

Saint Lawrence Island

Mount McKinley (20,320 feet)

YUKON RIVER

KUSKOKWIM RIVER

Denali National Park

SUST...

Ta...

Yukon Delta National Wildlife Refuge

Red Devil

Elmendorf A. F. B.

Mata...

Kenai

Eek

LAKE CLARK

Lake Clark N. P.

ILIAMNA LAKE

Clam Gulch

BERING SEA

ALEKNAGIK LAKE

Kenai Nation...

COOK INLET

King Salmon

Katmai National Park

Kodiak

BECHAROF LAKE

Kodiak Island

Attu Island

Novarupta Volcano

Kodiak National Wildlife Refuge

Chignik

Pavlof Volcano

Aleutian Islands

Kiska Island

MAP KEY

Admiralty Island	E12	Becharof Lake	E7	Elmendorf		Ketchikan	E12
Alaska Pipe Line	B8	Bering Sea	D3	Air Force Base	D8	King Salmon	E7
Alcan Highway	D10	Bering Strait	B,C5	Fairbanks	C9	Kiska Island	F1
Aleknagik Lake	E7	Candle	C6	Fort Richardson	D8	Kobuk Valley National	
Aleutian Islands	F,G1-6	Chichagof Island	E11	Fort Yukon	B9	Park	B7
Anchorage	D8	Chicken	C9	Gates of the Arctic		Kodiak	F8
Arctic Circle	B7	Chignik	F7	National Park	B8	Kodiak Island	F8
Arctic National Wildlife		Clam Gulch	E8	Glacier Bay National		Kodiak National Wildlife	
Refuge	B9	Coffman Cove	E12	Park	E11	Refuge	F8
Arctic Ocean	A9	Colville River	A7,8	Gulf of Alaska	E9,10	Kotzebue	B6
Attu Island	F1	Cook Inlet	E8	Iliamna Lake	E7	Koyukuk River	C7,8
Baranof Island	E11	Deadhorse	A8	Juneau	E11	Kuskokwim River	D7
Barrow	A7	Denali National Park	D8	Katmai National Park	E7	Lake Clark	E7
Beaver	B8	Eek	E6	Kenai	E8	Lake Clark	
		Eielson		Kenai Fjords National		National Park	E7
		Air Force Base	C9	Park	E8	Malaspina Glacier	D10

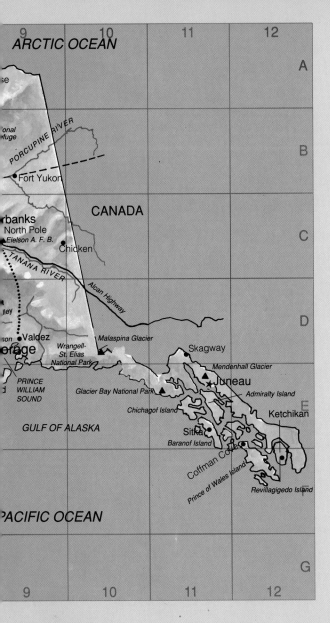

GLOSSARY

Arctic: The region north of the Arctic Circle

Arctic Circle: An imaginary line that passes through Alaska as it encircles the world

billion: A thousand million (1,000,000,000)

bush pilot: A pilot who flies people and supplies into remote areas

capital: A city that is the seat of government

capitol: The building in which a government meets

century: A 100-year period

climate: The typical weather of a region

coast: The land along a large body of water

fjord: A finger of the sea that extends inland

frontier: A place that has just started to become developed

kayak: A narrow Eskimo boat with a covered deck

million: A thousand thousand (1,000,000)

61

northern lights: A nighttime light display caused by activity on the sun; also called the aurora borealis

population: The number of people in a place

remote: Far from people or towns

totem pole: A carved wooden pole made by Northwest Coast Indians

tundra: A cold, treeless, rather flat region

umiak: An open Eskimo boat that is larger than a kayak

volcano: A mountain from which hot rock and other materials erupt

woolly mammoth: An elephant-like animal that died out long ago

PICTURE ACKNOWLEDGMENTS

Front cover, © George Hunter/**H. Armstrong Roberts**; 1, © Edmond Van Hoorick /**SuperStock**; 2, **Tom Dunnington**; 3, **© Tom Dietrich**; 4-5, **Tom Dunnington**; 6-7, © Mike Barlow/**Dembinsky Photo Assoc.**; 8, © Gregory Martin/**SuperStock**; 9 (top), **Courtesy of Hammond, Incorporated, Maplewood, New Jersey**; 9 (bottom), © Lael Morgan/**Tony Stone Images**; 10, © Stan Osolinski/**Dembinsky Photo Assoc.**; 11, © Rod Planck/**Dembinsky Photo Assoc.**; 12 (top), © Mike Barlow/**Dembinsky Photo Assoc.**; 12 (bottom), © C. Postmus/**Root Resources**; 13, © Mike Barlow/**Dembinsky Photo Assoc.**; 14, © Atchison/**Photri**; 15, © Mike Barlow/**Dembinsky Photo Assoc.**; 16, **Courtesy The Edward E. Ayer Collection, The Newberry Library, Chicago**; 18, **Stock Montage, Inc.**; 19, **Stock Montage, Inc.**; 20, **Alaska and Polar Regions Dept., University of Alaska Fairbanks/Historical Photograph Collection (60-959-19N)**; 21, **Alaska and Polar Regions Dept., University of Alaska Fairbanks/Hannah Call Photograph Collection (70-11-35N)**; 22, **AP/Wide World Photos**; 23, **AP/Wide World Photos**; 24, © Rod Stapleton/**Dembinsky Photo Assoc.**; 25, © Gregory Martin/**SuperStock**; 26, © Philip & Karen Smith/**Tony Stone Images**; 27 (top), **© Joan Dunlop**; 27 (bottom), **Alaska Division of Tourism**; 28, **© Bob & Ira Spring**; 29 (left), © Brent Winebrenner/**mga/Photri**; 29 (right), © Margo Taussig Pinkerton/**N E Stock Photo**; 30, © George Riley/**N E Stock Photo**; 31 (left), © John Warden/**Tony Stone Images**; 31 (right),© Grant Klotz/**N E Stock Photo**; 32-33, © Grant Klotz/**N E Stock Photo**; 34, © Raymond G. Barnes/**Tony Stone Images**; 35 (left), © D. C. Lowe/**SuperStock**; 35 (right), © George Hunter/**H. Armstrong Roberts**; 36, © C. W. Biedel/**Photri**; 37, © Jim Schwabel/**N E Stock Photo**; 38, © John Warden/**Tony Stone Images**; 39, © Grant Klotz/**N E Stock Photo**; 40, © Olaf Soot/**Tony Stone Images**; 41, © Kevin Schaefer/**Tom Stack & Associates**; 42, © Clyde H. Smith/**N E Stock Photo**; 43 (left), © Lawrence Migdale/**Tony Stone Images**; 43 (right), **© Bob & Ira Spring**; 44, © Pinkerton/Arend/**N E Stock Photo**; 45, © Paul Damien/**Tony Stone Images**; 46, **University of Alaska, photo by Dennis Brack**; 47, **Alaska and Polar Regions Dept., University of Alaska Fairbanks/Historical Photograph Collection (83-209-76N)**; 48, **Alaska and Polar Regions Dept., University of Alaska Fairbanks/Charles Keim Photograph Collection (67-44-3N)**; 49, **Alaska and Polar Regions Dept., University of Alaska Fairbanks/Charles E. Bunnell Collection (73-66-33N)**; 50, **Alaska and Polar Regions Dept., University of Alaska Fairbanks/Historical Photograph Collection (83-41-1)**; 53, © Rob Stapleton/**Dembinsky Photo Assoc.**; 54 (bottom), **AP/Wide World Photos**; 54-55 (top), **© Alan Landau Photography**; 55, **© Les Anderson**; 56 (top), **Courtesy Flag Research Center, Winchester, Massachusetts 01890**; 56 (bottom), © Joe Atchison/**Photri**; 57 (top), **Alaska Division of Tourism**; 57 (middle), © Chase Swift/**Tom Stack & Associates**; 57 (bottom), © Anthony Mercieca/**Root Resources**; 58, **Alaska and Polar Regions Department, Elmer E. Rasmuson Library, University of Alaska Fairbanks/Charles Bunnell Collection**; 60-61, **Tom Dunnington**; back cover, © SharkSong, M. Kazmers/**Dembinsky Photo Assoc.**

INDEX

Page numbers in boldface type indicate illustrations.

ABOUT THE AUTHOR

Dennis Brindell Fradin is the author of 150 published children's books. His works for Childrens Press include the Young People's Stories of Our States series, the Disaster! series, and the Thirteen Colonies series. Dennis is married to Judith Bloom Fradin, who taught high-school and college English for many years. She is now Dennis's chief researcher. The Fradins are the parents of two sons, Anthony and Michael, and a daughter, Diana. Dennis graduated from Northwestern University in 1967 with a B.A. in creative writing, and has lived in Evanston, Illinois, since that year.

DATE DUE			
4S 4L			

13674

979.8
FRA

Fradin, Dennis B.

Alaska